Dedication

To that Primal Energy of my Spiritual Mother who gives me the regular strength to fight, embrace and conquer the ordeals of Life with the love and loss of Red…..And to All such Abhayas, Nirbhayas & Fearless Women of the World, brutally treated daily, killed and raped by the ageless guillotine of patriarchy to be re-christened in death as the Rising Spirit of Womanhood, the Genesis of All Creation. Poetic prayers to transform drastically this signal of our times.

WOMAN : *A Tribute*

I am a Woman, an amazing tree of life
a stunning follicle of immensity
fruit, flower and foliage of being and un-being
of all that breathes inside and outside ---

I am a Woman of wise wistfulness
a re-building after all erosion and sighs
the rage and calm of the flowing river
ravage and rise of the seedling in hide ---

I am a Woman born in the eye of a storm
a cardinal rib that protects your soul
a tingle of ebullience in ruddy tears
invincible joy defying claws of woes---

I am a Woman of continuity unstoppable
despite all lies I enrich with truth of knowledge
I mount to kiss the stars and delve into the deep
I remain the womb, the cell and over-arching pledge ---

I am a Woman holding the enormity of living
it is hard to read the reigning riddles I clasp
for I am your genesis, your love and hate forever
your creation and annihilation in dawn and dusk ---

Laksmisree Banerjee has been consistent in her pursuit of poetry and of the mostly painful secrets of the human condition. In this book *The Red Woman* she gives eloquent expression to her identification with the marginalized and unfortunate women in life as well as history. But these are not just wailing on the plight of women but also poetic attempts to awaken women and instill life into their half-charred hearts and rebellion in their muted brains. I wish her all success in life".

Prof. K. Satchidanandan
Eminent Poet & Scholar, Fmr. Secy. Sahitya Akademi, Delhi

"Poet Laksmisree Banerjee's arresting Collection *The Red Woman* is a potent tour-de-force through womanhood, culminating in a meticulous polemic rebellion. The purpose of her main character is to dispel the tired myth that a woman's value lies in her physicality, age and 'virtue'. The Red Woman of Banerjee's imagination is defiant, visceral and her vividness and endurance takes great pride in destroying all stereotypes. This angel-human is not defined by false histories but is metaphorically all women, in all incarnations, both symbolic and literal. Her demand to be counted and not ignored, is universal; she will no longer subjugate herself because others wish her erased or controlled. It takes a great mind and deep familiarity with history to evoke such a temple to women, who are often reduced to typecasting and predictability and Banerjee is that devoted and knowing writer. She delineates those fierce, quiet moments where we know we are so much more for our womanhood with our ability to survive, as perceived within these searing pages".

Candice Louisa Daquin
Eminent Poet & Sr. Editor & Publisher,
Indie Blu Publishing, Ed. Partner Raw Earth Ink,
The Pine Cone Review,
Tint Journal & Parcham Literary Magazine.USA

"Laksmisree Banerjee's ***The Red Woman*** proves that even in this twelfth collection, she has lost none of her energy and passion but has rather gained in maturity and confidence. Banerjee's inimitable voice continues to challenge both complacency and patriarchy. Fire and the colour Red are powerful symbols that burn in her poems and remain intensely personal, while also connecting with the reader because of the universality and immediacy of the issues raised".

Dr. Debjani Chatterjee
MBE & Fellow of the Royal Society of Literature
Eminent Poet, Writer & Creative Arts Psychotherapist, UK

The Red Woman

Laksmisree Banerjee

Foreword By
Bashabi Fraser

BLACK EAGLE BOOKS
Dublin, USA | Bhubaneswar, India

Black Eagle Books
USA address:
7464 Wisdom Lane
Dublin, OH 43016

India address:
E/312, Trident Galaxy, Kalinga Nagar,
Bhubaneswar-751003, Odisha, India

E-mail: info@blackeaglebooks.org
Website: www.blackeaglebooks.org

First International Edition Published by
Black Eagle Books, 2025

THE RED WOMAN
by **Laksmisree Banerjee**

Foreword by Bashabi Fraser

Copyright © **Laksmisree Banerjee**

All rights reserved. No part of this publication may be reproduced, stored in a retrieval system, or transmitted, in any form or by any means, electronic, mechanical, photocopying, recording or otherwise without the prior permission of the publisher.

Cover & Interior Design: Ezy's Publication

ISBN- 978-1-64560-637-6 (Paperback)
Library of Congress Control Number: 2024952857

Printed in the United States of America

Foreword

Bashabi Fraser

They shut me up in Prose
As when a little Girl
They put me in the Closet
Because they liked me 'still'
                                -Emily Dickinson

Laksmisree Banerjee brings patriarchy to account in her new collection of poems, *The Red Woman*. In her impressive career as a poet covering three and a half decades, Laksmisree's distinctive voice is evident in this, her twelfth poetry collection. She joins a long line of our foremothers in poets like Christina Rossetti, Emily Dickinson, Mina Loy, Sylvia Plath and more recently, poets of colour like Kamala Das and Maya Angelou, capturing the feminine predicament both in her home country, India and globally, in poems that are imbued with her empathy with those who are/have been wronged, discarded, neglected and abused now and through the centuries.

The collection begins with 'The Red Woman' in *Sonagachi*, the godforsaken red-light district of Kolkata where a woman whose dismal seedy life belies her cheap outward glitter, as the tragedy of her whole existence is emphasized by her eternal entrapment:

> wandering through the unknown maze
>   of winding ways
>   ever lost....

The universality of the woman's predicament is captured as the poet narrator identifies with each woman she commemorates and/or celebrates through space and time:

> like you, I have found myself,
> lived in alien lands as my own,
> sprouting with new leaves
> in painful transplantation,
> geo-spaces and temporality,...
> in centuries of undeterred womanhood
> ('Dear Woman').

The pathos of the caged-bird image of one who has forgotten how to sing, is recalled in 'Silence', while the search for hidden treasure in an oyster is commemorated in the lonely figure walking along the seashore or sitting with the waves lapping at her feet in 'Thirst'. However, these women, silenced or isolated, 'grow in death' as they affirm in one voice,

> my silence is your delusion
> my voicelessness your hallucination.

The subaltern speaks and does so collectively from across the globe

> from Egypt to Indonesia
> from Amazon to America
> from Somalia to India
> from England to Kenya.
> One recalls Mina Loy's words,
> Our Universe
> Is only
> A colorless onion
> You derobe
> Sheath by sheath.

As the poet in Laksmisree concedes that we are at the mercy of the dominant power in poem after poem, yet something remains beneath those robes, a dignity that assails the abuser with a pungency recalling

> A disheartening odour
> About your nervy hands.
>
> (from Songs of Joannes, verse X)

The trials and tribulations women suffer, paradoxically lend them their undeniable identity, 'in red, green and pure gold' ('I Grow in Death'), making them discernible in their glowing vibrant colours. However, against their vibrancy, there is also the sharply contrasted image of the child widow, bereft of colour, shrouded in white before her youth has blossomed, 'a widow/ for life' in 'She'.

Laksmisree is both universal and personal, as she recalls her grandmother's excruciating humiliation imposed by a patriarchal familial set up in 'Timeless Sin'. As a girl, the grand matriach

> Was chained in darkness in the cowshed

> Barred from sunlight
> Four days a month ---

because a harsh, insensitive society decreed that
It was a crime for her to bleed
Like it was for her to be a girl.

The mother's unfulfilled aspirations are captured in a poignant corollary drawn between her and the sensitive Anne Frank:

> My Mother perhaps was born
>   on the same day as Anne Frank…

and just as her young life was blighted, the mother's

> …dreams lived throughout her
> full life, forever unfulfilled. ('Of Mother and Trees')

Yet, the woman's spirit remains indomitable in Laksmisree's confirmation of her divine power. Like Maya Angelou, she can see beyond the 'bitter, twisted lies' of history recorded by the dominant voices, but she will 'rise' and continue to rise. In a similar vein, Laksmisree asserts,
  I shine in your translucent third eye
    Glimmering through my lows and highs…
  I am your beaming face in ignited sanctity….
    A pantheistic presence that rolls through all things….
    Changing with the seasons, seas and azure ('The Divine Feminine') -
  dancing to the universal rhythm of life itself, 'ignited' by righteous anger, sensitized by the poet's

inherent empathy, all of which are expressively captured in her poems. The 'vigilant third eye' is forever awake in Laksmisree's poetry as she walks with the prostitute, remembers the child widow, the smothered, silenced, shunned, isolated or lonely woman, the girl denied her playtime days or the mother with unfulfilled aspirations. The poet feels their pain while she knows and reveres their role as nurturers and sustainers of life and light, the very symbols of continuity and sustenance. The poems in *The Red Woman* will not be shut up in a closet and lie 'still', for they sing of women. They will sing to them and to those who value and love their grandmothers, mothers, wives, daughters and sisters, bringing the hope of freedom to lives which have been resurrected and revitalized with a reverence that Laksmisree has shown to womankind in this collection.

Professor Emerita of English and Creative Writing
Director, Scottish Centre of Tagore Studies (ScoTs)
Editor-in-Chief, *Gitanjali and Beyond*, United Kingdom

Author's Note

This Collection of my Poems is an Ode to Womanhood, celebrating and embracing all the features of fullness and contradictions that make her a complete being. This cornucopia of female, feminine and feminist attributes of wholeness, struck me as a potent starting point, when I discovered it, having written my poem *The Red Woman*, which is the first poem in this compendium. The word and conceptualization of the colour "Red" of course began with the phrase of "a red light area" denoting the oldest trade of the world, namely the sex-trade, a painful result of patriarchy promoted by licentious men at the cost of hapless women who continue to surrender to male lust without much of an option. It is also a fact that the natural reverence for a Woman/ Mother is intrinsically connected to the worship of the Mother Goddess Durga and all her manifestations through diverse regions of India, for which the soil of a prostitute's home from a red-light area has to be collected, thus accentuating the incongruity of our traditions connected to the intrinsic purity of womanhood. Of course, I must admit that a rainbow of truths invaded and painted my mind while writing these poems through the last one year. The predominance of the Red Colour, its efficacy and usage, is interwoven in my poetic fabric with its equally anomalous connotations of oppression and vibrancy, sensuality and spirituality, violence and tranquility, hatred and love, ferocity and calmness, radiance and pallor etc., which are features central to female lives and male and female nature as well. Hence I believe that this Collection is not a totally Feminist one with virulence at its core;--rather it is about women as total human beings (in a larger world), who are full of love, strength and fortitude, asking for understanding and caring through all their ordeals and attainments in life. Though most of these poems are new, this anthology also includes a few selected poems from my earlier books which contribute to making it my plea for a holistic vision and reality of a better world of companionship and gender equality.

In the meantime the brutal murder and rape of a young female doctor within the premises of the well-known R.G. Kar Hospital in my home city of Kolkata on 9th August 2024 has sent shock waves not only across India but the entire world. After the gruesome rape and murder of *Nirbhaya* (re-christened as the Fearless one) in Delhi 2012, this recent ruthless murder and rape of a young woman in Kolkata (re-christened *Abhaya* or the Unafraid One) has brought about an unprecedented Social Revolution and Churning for Gender Justice and Gender Equality across the globe. Hence this Book of my Poems is dedicated to the *Abhayas* & *Nirbhayas* of the world (the last segment has a Tribute of five poems) so that humankind sits up once again to think seriously and also act for abolishing dogmas and cruelty to create a better world for Women, the Race of Mothers and the Genesis of all Creation.

As this book goes to the press, I recall that famous line by Poet Florence Howe *"To be a woman is to be human & to be a woman poet is to encompass the difficult world"*. Looking forward to empathy and happy reading and of course a Publication which I believe would resonate across the world of our communities of friends, thinkers, readers and writers.

(Prof. Dr.) Laksmisree Banerjee
May 2024, Kolkata & Jamshedpur, India

CONTENTS

The Red Woman	01
Dear Woman	06
Antique Shadows	09
Tryst with Tagore : Kadombori Returns	13
Silence	16
Thirst	18
I Grow in Death	20
Hungry Glitz	22
Scars : Burnt Woman	23
Fire of a New Woman	25
Red Empress	27
She	29
Timeless Sin	30
Rose in Tatters	31
Sita or Sati	32
Sky	34
Of Mother and Trees	36
Stifled Scream	37
Unborn Kill	39
Sindoor	40
Mother : A Memory	42
Tinsel Heart	44
The Divine Feminine	45
Veiled Chimera	46
Moon Spindles of Singhbhum	47
Eternal Mother	49
Lakshman Rekha	50
Queen Nature	52
Red Rose Calling	54
Mother and Child in No Man's Land	56
Primordial Woman	59

Fire of Yagnaseni	60
Red Bloom	63
Fire Ball	65
Devi – Manushi	67
Grandma's Wrap	69
Blood Streams	71
Soul and Sham	73
Dark Red Spring	75
Searching Home	77
Woman or Wood Nymph	79
That Red Glistening Edge	81
Roses Arise	83
Strange Parting	84
Cigarettes	87
Scarred Moon	89
Womanhood	90
Red Queen of Nemesis	92
Memories	95
Nirbhaya	97
Denouement	99
The Desecrated Mother	101
Unhappy Independence Day	103
Renaissance after Her Martyrdom	105
We Rise with Her	107
Glossary	108

"Light, O where is the light?---
Let not the hours pass by in the dark
Kindle the lamp of love with thy life"

       Rabindranath Tagore
       from *Gitanjali*

"Two roads diverged in a wood
And I took the less traversed by
And that made all the difference"

       Robert Frost
       from *The Road Not Taken*

The Red Woman

I am the red woman
my home is in *Sonagachi*
wandering through the unknown maze
of winding ways
ever lost
through red lit areas of my crushed heart
sighted, blighted always
in the ruddy shades of pain
often in bridal chambers or
in elite lounges or nocturnal bars
of piercing love-cradles
yet forever in refuge and refuse
in lusty dimness of male stench
my home always in *Sonagachi*
the waste-bin of the world ---

I am the red woman
I arise in darkness embracing
the green gold of trees
I bathe in the lilting shimmer
of the moonlit breeze
but my flesh, the wracked crevices
of my body and soul
so often shredded, battered
tattered in secrecy
splinters of perjury

played around by you
the known and unknown
as my spirit wings through
the beauty of the ether
I become the forgetful fairy
yet in cringe and fury against
your cruel sport with my womanliness
my home always in *Sonagachi*
the waste-bin of the world---

I am the red woman
wearing so many shrouds
of the goddess or the mother
the caretaker, the sister, wife
daughter or the lover or simply slave
in the garden, bed or bower
forever the whore in unwillingness
breathing in blankness of being
a wincing void, an erasure of my own self
in robotic tending of my ashen flames
sleeping, cleaning, giving or caressing
in recognition or repulsion
I am Nature still in forced coitus
with primordial savagery
bestiality masked in varied forms
playing chicanery with me
reduced to a tennis ball or a doll
my home always in *Sonagachi*
the waste-bin of the world ---

I am the red woman
the fireball thumping in me
now with my volcanic redness

the inwardness of luminous awakening
I shout with bellowing faith
the weeping resonance of the centuries
with purity of my earth and empyrean
I shout, I resonate, don't you hear?
you are the whore
not I
you have sold your soul
not I
you have revelled in perfidy
not I
you have traded in lust
not I
you are the harlot
not I
be it in glitzy *Soho* of London
be it in the commodity of
glass-cased breasts and vaginas
sold in *De Wallen* of Amsterdam
be it in *Reeparbahn Strasse* that street
of putrid licence in Hamburg
be it in *Mello* garish areas of Malta
be it in pizzazz *Heeramandi* of Lahore
be it in gaudy *Kamathipura* of Mumbai
be it in tawdry *Sonagachi* of Kolkata
you are the whore
not I
you have created oceans of blood and tears
not I
I am the red woman
my home ever encaged in *Sonagachi*
the waste-bin of your world ---

You carve my images of *Ma Durga*
with the clay of my muddied home
you swim with hardened recklessness
in the divine ambience of my *Shakti*
only till your festive mood lasts
then you drown me
in your ceremonies of immersion
as my memory flows down the river
you kill me after your orgy is done
in labyrinths of carcasses of your doomsday
you use my womb to create your children
who you can never love
but dump in your fabricated orphanages
called homes
you are the whore
not I
as I remain sanitized
in my waste-bin of the world ---

I am the red woman
clad in my red *Benarasi* sari
my hair swamped with red *sindoor*
insignia of your patriarchy
my feet and palms inundated
with red colours of your nakedness
my forehead darkened with that ruddy orb
the emblem of lawful prostitution
my body and soul soaked in blood
as I linger on for the white light
of my own eyes, years and immortal tears
to fill my nest with tender illumination ---

I am the red woman
the sweltering star, your cosmic progenitor
as I wait for my glittering lamps
reverberating signs of the multiverse
I become the red *ardhanarishwar*
the deified androgynous warrior to chastise and chasten
in my waste-bin home of the world in *Sonagachi*...

I am the red woman
waiting to explode as the sunflower
in yellow transcendence
in forests of wild flames
in conflagrations of softness
the red rose in wrath and bloom
as my home in *Sonagachi* waits ever like me
to filter out the briny seas of treachery
to purify you smudged souls of the world
mark my words and acts of ablution
I am the Redness of your Mother's womb
I am the Red Woman with the third eye
I am the Red Woman of ten armed alms
I am the Red Woman of your desire and worship
I birth your sons and daughters with fondness
I am the Red Woman of love and vengeance
I am the Red Woman of cinders and milk
shining ever in reincarnated harvests of bullied bullion
with a Red Dot of Love still on my forehead
blazing in your murk with my turmeric sunshine
look how the waste-bin of the world is soon washed out---

Dear Woman

Dear Woman,
we hang from the boughs of
the same tree of un-tasted succulence
along zig-zag tracks of unknown tangles
as the bride-calling Bird
awakens me mellifluously
in my bridal attire and bower
entangled long ago in the breeze of
fully unfulfilled dreams ---

enmeshed in the strains of crimson
lasting lost desires in dense forests
ages before we knew each other
as sisters in no man's land
or perhaps eons before
we danced hand in hand in no woman's land,
brewing in interludes of scorching coffee breaks
myself already poisoned by
the fruit of knowledge
still clinging to our age-old elysium
beyond its gates of banishment ---

the golden clouds have melted since
into the delirium of darkness of nocturnal trees,
much before you ripened into
the fallen mango

splattered on ground
with rancid juice of unrequited love...

I lived through this weary story of survival
much before you my dear sister
I knew the silken reverie
we had always woven
to play our roles wrapped around
in our dead silk worms
still emitting glow in living deaths ---

I hemmed into my life of
history's blank pages with
bitter sweetness
a frolicsome masquerade
now flooding across with
cascades of tearful amnesia
perhaps much before you
perhaps much later than her ---

but now, like you, I have found myself,
lived in alien lands as my own,
sprouting with new leaves
in painful transplantation,
geo-spaces and temporality,
rivers, rocks and seas
now bland in the sameness
of dark and light,
dear sister we are very much alike
in our vain equipoise of
a suave, customary compromise...

yes we are now united and ignited
in our belligerent making,
in centuries of undeterred womanhood
sculpted in artistry through hammer and anvil,
as wisely beautiful as the singing river
breaking its way through stones into the sea,
drenched in dreams yet not soggy ---

you and I the sturdy all-encompassing banyan tree
not seeking but giving shade
as strong as the earth
as omniscient as the ether
as inflamed as the fire
as inspired as the wind
as amorous as desire
as fierce as the hurricane
as soft as blooming love
as liberal as the sky ---

We celebrate here and now
our womanhood timeless,
our hot-springs welling out
of the flinty no man's land,
our greenery piping out of crevices
of jagged elemental rocks
we have made our quilts, woven our yarns
to clothe the dark secrets of the world ---

Now we stand together
bare, unfurled
at the still point of history ---

Antique Shadows

She remembered entering the past
in that forty-roomed crumbling *haveli*
a gnarled, ruinous object de art
from a bygone feudal age----
she entered without a name
but with a role ,
a golden net, a trophy
a fluid maidenhood meshed
in a hazy foliage of dreams---

The red velvet would stretch endlessly
like a bloody river
from the threshold
where she entered
till her envisaged pyre,
so she was told by elders
with extreme concern
for her lifetime of wellbeing,
her present, her past
her future, her forever---

She was reconstructed
with finery, clamping jewellery
a good status-symbol
for private use and public display---
She went through

dark staircases, eerie alleys
rusty bars, hollows, nooks
communication mazes,
shadowy webs of gloom---

Locked within the wintry rooms
with peel-off plasters,
sombre dim lights, vacuities
decayed ancestral paintings,
broken chandeliers, unused libraries,
crumbling, jammed teak doors,
squeaky windows forever closed,
with cobweb jungles, dusty proscriptions
empty spaces barred from sunlight---.

She need not have looked
for the exit ----- she was told,
loyal slaves and escorts were at call
in case she needed
to see the light of day
old, unread books, binoculars
her only friends, scowling bison horns,
petrifying tiger-visage, eyes crucified
macabre foggy mirrors on guard
transfixed on lack-lustre old walls ---

The knotty *bael* tree in
the central courtyard
with no fruits but leaves
for appeasing household gods
the *Brahmadaitya* half-god, half-demon
living in the tree of hearsay
a protector, a police for
the deadening heritage
with its mouldering ramparts

Ten acres of encircling
garden with screeching owls, bats,
barking dogs, forbidding moats,
howling jackals, uncanny hooting,
a no-man's land except
her own forsaken woman-land
in alien despair of a house away from home
a limitless boundary
as far as her eyes could see

The deep, mossy, circular
pond with hyacinth-strangulated
water in dead stillness
tall steeples of coconut
trees with dishevelled
monstrous hairy branches
casting long shadows of
tired setting suns on
the stiffening borders

The clayey loam,
the marshy girdle,
the mire on dilapidated statues
with nettles, formidable barriers
wrecked dykes and drains around
the rotting fish, the algae
fetid leaves, vegetables
the endless circle of courtyards
had the stench of bygone days---

She learnt strange arts while
the caged parrot made empty chatter
making sandalwood paste, stirring

in hot smoky kitchens with fireballs of wet eyes
with *brahmin* cooks making *brahmin bhogs*
in firewood *unoons,* she pottering useless
in silks and clutches of adornments
in closeted freedom of female glory
as doors would open, lattices removed
for guests to enter, inspect and laud
the newest toy in her in-laws home---

Tryst with Tagore: Kadombori Returns

Dear my Apollonian Krishna, my Beloved Poet *Robi*---
You have sculpted me immutable through ages
Your immaculate mallet of untold love and grief
Our romance and rebellion of mute roses
Illumines the corridors of human renascence---

Our love a flowing stream of rock-hard permanence
I recall so with my moist vision of cataracts
Bursting in the veins of our red brick cage
Our *nondan kanon* torn asunder in bristles
Drowned, desiccated, forlorn now in dogma---

A brittle arid estuary guzzling our river
Across many oceans of relentless tears
Wading through domestic intrigue
In feudal darkness all unduly knotted
Slowly drowning my passion in silence
In the surges of my love for you
Through ages of timeless union
Unseen, unknown, cruel, cryptic
Forever ending in cascades of separation ---

Yet reincarnating through uncountable births
Through illimitable summers and winters
Born and reborn in shimmers of midnight turmoil
And often in the sunshine of your amorous eyes

Your eyes the cosmic sea merging with my horizon
Just for you, just for you, just for you ---

I lie throttled in the poison of perfidy
My froth of feelings ends in suffocation
So many lives I have lived for you alone
So many births I have bloomed for you alone
So many deaths I have endured for you alone
So many loves I have borne for you alone
So many opium dreams I have towed for you alone
Myself the heavenly *parijat* flowering in doom for you alone--

I still gain transcendence in your honeyed touch
My tumescence, budding and falling lifeless on ground
Your intense clutch has enthralled me through the millennia
My past births, deaths, youth and age all lost
Lost in the high tides of our nectarine love
In the bedecked crib of cruel codes of conduct
Fulfilled forever yet eternally unrequited ---

Dear my Beloved *Kobi* I have resurged so many times
In the thorny bower of our love un-satiated
And died through so many more births and deaths
Of hallowed agony and ecstasy in boldness
Along the cusp of a nettled society
Through untold illusions and insights
For you and you alone ---

But you remain in stillnes my Seer-Bard
Ever distant, ever breathing into my breath
Far and near, though mouth to mouth
In atemporal resuscitation
Our never-ending fairytale of history---

Ever tangled, locked in shards of our reverie
My withering self cupped in your palms
You my cruel enchanter forever fleeing through mists
To create new seas of prancing waves
Of undercurrents, embraces and lambent tears
My amorous drizzle, wrenched heart, my fears
My faces, lives, youth, cravings through years
My frozen ephemera in our shrine of posterity
In the pyramid of sacred passion
Etched timelessly in the sands of forbidden love
In which we carouse forever in fleeting breeze---

(**Kadombori: Tagore's Sister-in-law and his Muse;   Kobi: Poet)

Silence

This bird-cage in muteness
how it looks like a bell sans chime
hanging in mellow light ---

I sit along the sea side
in the verandah of
my pensive thoughts

the dwindling rays of the sun
fall underground
to plummeting death

far away they run amok
dangling arrows of skewed
minds make them run

helter-skelter for shelter
as hungry mouths gobble
cries of wailing children

floating corpses of my soul
rise from the depths of
dark subterranean sorrows

along lengthening shadows
of the night of sandy desertion
till the finality of extinct hours

silence arrives like a blanket
after the explosions
when the day is done

as skeletons sleep in hiding
dead secrets of
bruised womanhood ---

Thirst

The brown wilted leaves dusky in whorls
cuddled in parched mud
can hardly breathe
some of them still hang
on twigs of the crooked tree
with a bent broken spine
unquenched forever
along the thirsty salt-laden shores
of an orange-grey sundown ---

the emaciated flowers gasping on ground
trapeze in a dance of death
fiercely rolling in a wayward wind
stuffed heartlessness invites
the dark clandestine night ---

I sit lonely with the warrior waves
thrashing my feet frail
with endless walking along rude fences
in search of sea shells with live molluscs
hoping to find a live oyster
breathing a brilliant pearl to hide
a shelter from the tradesmen out there ---

I wait for the drowsy sun
to drop into my lap lovingly
for a tranquil sleep ---

yet nothingness is all
no scintillating pearl
no warm love in sight
no quench of thirst
as the sun dives into
the abysmal cold waters
leaving behind the fathomless night
myself lost in an infinity of betrayal
in search for that light!

I Grow in Death

You split my tongue
you slit my throat
you slash my wings
you axe my foliage
you drink me dry ---

my silence is your delusion
my voicelessness your hallucination
embers of my soul in wrath
my body a cemetery
of speaking ashes in full bloom
you smell the purgatorial ambrosia
of my daring incensed fragrance ---

from Egypt to Indonesia
from Amazon to America
from Somalia to India
from England to Kenya
my trails of travails at home and abroad
make me red, green and pure gold
I revel in my firewood-pain
a ruptured spirit ever unflagging
my gullet cut resonates endlessly
a croaking frog dancing in the rain ---

my split tongue now
breeds poison of enchantment
the serpent of your creation
enamoring so many of you
perhaps a snapdragon ready to eat
a rose resurrected as a gobbling cactus
spiky, unforgiving, a twisted cobra
sculpted through your tyranny ---

as you cut so I grow
more you suck more I flow
you make me bleed
a river of the cold billows
my life eternal in death
as my skeletal branches flail
they splice you
lacerate you ---

I rise in my new vision
you fall in your remorseless illusion
my living death now my azure
I am the bird of love
a snake in the sky ---

Hungry Glitz

Grey fog had settled silently
with catty paws after sundown
across the clandestine bend
of Park Street and Free School Street
in the dim lights criss-crossing
the glitzy arena enjoying their regular joke ---

A blanket of dark miasma
gasping with cold life as
the wintry garment of mist
wrapped around the shrivelled body
chewing crumbs with street dogs
as a hungry glitz lit up her red-light stage---

The red woman in black shimmers
with pallid innards forsaken
ran breathlessly down her dirty staircase
to scatter her fake glimmer
her outcaste glamour among hungry men
to stand and catch her belching prey ---

The moon winked from afar
as she stood by the road side
of zipping sedans along swanky hotels
bars with tongues of flames baking lust
liberty and license in the cauldron
questions thrown from laughing stars
who was whose prey anyway?

SCARS: Burnt Woman

(Based on an Actual Incident----myself and my young kid- - Victims of a Tata Steel Fire Tragedy of 1989- the Founders Day, 150th Birth Anniversary of Jamshedji N. Tata in which Hundreds of Women and Children of Sr. Executives were injured and killed in the VIP Gallery)

No, my scars could never
melt into the blue, they seethed
and breathed till

They have come to blossom
as strength stronger
than truth

As beauty more beautiful
than flowers, as fire more
incandescent than bridal lava

As armour more formidable
than death and insouciant
fury of destiny

I shall remember the way
you took your way out
into a new future

Discarding me like
a burnt log or some sterile
dirt of the desert

Or a brittle parchment
not worth the deciphering

Or some dried up rose
smothered in cinders ---

Yet I thank that unknown grace
For my tears hardened
Into granite chips,
For the flames that taught me
The lessons of love and life
For his burning godhood
And your ice-cold abandonment---

Fire of A New Woman

(Based on a Real Life Personal Fire Tragedy inside the Tata Steel Works in Jamshedpur, India, during the Founder's Day Celebrations of 1989, in which our VIP Gallery was burnt to ashes with Hundreds Killed and Maimed , as fire-crackers were used with criminal negligence---myself and my kid / only girl & child, being severely injured and incapacitated for 3 years with painful and critical burn surgeries----the Tragedy has been put under wraps ever since....my Book of Poems FIRE OFFERINGS with the Title & Foreword by Keki Daruwalla, was published soon after)__

From the scarlet bougainvillea
of my sizzling burns
to the black rose
of your betrayal
I found my way
a tear-lit avenue ---

I found the rock
I found the soil
I found the word
I found the song
I found the breath
of my sighs in that inferno
sizzling in my wounds
my soul boiling
in a beaker of flames

dreaming those other lives
we had spent in that ether of amnesia ---

You left me at day break
casting me aside coldly
myself an empty cup
of a dead conflagration ---

You found your new sangfroid
I found the darkness of fire
the light of knowledge---

Red Empress

I walked in as the empress of red glitter
Across the fenced threshold_
The toothy wooden jaws of red perjury
That pretty rose colour of violence
A barred entrance momentarily opened up
Of that crumbling heritage mansion
Hiding the blood of centuries ---

A *Lakshman Rekha*, a forbidding line of chastity
I entered tip-toing across this line of control
My feet bathed with blood-spills of *alta* and milk
With white lily dreams in my red weeping eyes
Though unable to decipher the hidden ruddiness
The cloaked red of the heart and womb in shards
Scooped out with claws of filth in secrecy---

I was a prized possession, a silken plastic
A glossy trophy with statuesque silence
A pretty doll for a perfect house- décor
Wrapped in the blood of an inherited red *banarasi*
Chained in adornments of flashy lightnings
With a red sun blazing on my forehead
My feet and palms painted with the colour of cruelty
In the fleshy blood- red of the *alta* and *mehendi*

I recall that red velvet on which my reddened feet tread
Myself like countless queens of antiquity in red brocade
A millennium of stress and trauma- trajectories
Tears of gore flooded my river banks
Avalanches of snowy pain deluged hillsides
And washed clean with weeping holiness
The carefully quilted stories of red womanhood ---

As I entered the infinite golden cage of red
With bandaged blood flowing through eternities
Oozing in homes, fields, roads, *havelis*, hovels, in harness
With open and closed spaces of asphyxiation drowned in semen
Across the carnal Time-Space continuum of heart and womb
My flushed dreams of sunken roses rose in carnage
Till my red *bindi* of love erupted into an inferno
My third eye opened in flames of my
sixth sense of devastation
To re-kindle and re-configure this Red Civilization ---

SHE

Married off on her eighth birthday
She hardly knew what
That dark red orb
Staining her forehead like blood
Meant.

She heard the bells ringing
Within a few years
Jingling with her jewels
And knew that it was springtime
That it was the happiest
Season of blossoming
In her life.

But suddenly the cruel
High tide ebbed,
The efflorescence waned off
Into extinction,
Into the agony of white.

As she was told that
She was a widow
For life.

Timeless Sin

My grandmother
Was chained in darkness in the cowshed
Barred from sunlight
Four days a month ---

It was a crime for her to bleed
Like it was for her to be a girl---

The fifth day, when she
Came out of the cold stench
She was purified,
Cleansed of Nature with cow dung and
Cascades of chilly Ganga water
Poured out of the bucket
On her trembling head and body---

Strangling her every month
With pneumonia ---

Rose in Tatters

I am a red bride of fluent agony
Touching your white heart
With my satin feathers
A scorching blush
Melting in your fire
A flash of softness wrapped
In blistering blood
With a pure ice-clad soul ---

Aching tumescence as we merge
Blossoming in twinge that sustains
Your vernal spikes which lacerate me
While milky loftiness
Fermented in unseen clogs
Placates and swaddles me
Heals and washes me
In apparitions of beauty
Yet the tingling tangle of truth in twain
Ever remains speaking in vain---

Awaiting that instant of nothingness
When our clock stops ticking
As you let me slip to ground easily
With silky vehemence from your palm
In holy tatters---

Sita or Sati

Born in fire
inured
deeply wound
in so-called love
I, in flaming chromosomes
linked with the lynched
natal bond---

Bred as a fire-girl,
a blazing rhododendron
in debris of dying embers
though schooled
naturally for the fire-rites
in covert constraints
of the yielding essences
of girlhood---

Taught to cower
along the fissures
of pain in prayers
along fake lines
of girly social norms
along prescriptions,
an *agnipariksha*
igniting every
moment of every
ash-laden breath
till the last one---

the edge
Pushed by a crying mother
as herself driven
to slice me off
from her bruised
umbilical cord
into the hungry
red ocean---

And then into
the vortex of *mantras*
savage drum beats
the melancholic
dissonance of
the nuptial *shehnai* drone
the dancing pyrotechnics
cacophony of customs
without salvage
the last rites complete
sacramental shrieks
with loud conch shells---

Sacrificial chants of
the *sindoor* ceremony
with blind smoky fire
the ultimate witness
myself lying in state
like the bleeding sunset
a dubious spectacle
drowning slowly in the night
a wounded red pieta
in the dark colours of
a make-believe whiteness---

Sky

She kept
   her home
      cosy,
The table laid,
   the teapoy
      ready and rosy.

Snug and aesthetic,
   her domestic
      hold,
a canopy of blazing
   lights of love in
      darkness.

Patchworks of flashy
   blues, greens,
      flowers red,
ostentatious elephants,
   inverted horses
      embroidered.

Faces with red *bindi* between
   cold dreamy eyes,
      cosmetic
lashes and groomed tresses
   edging painted
      red lips.

Showcases, lamps,
  crystals and dinner
    displays
dim with candles
  always awaiting
    the sun.

When the storm
  broke in,
    she
looked through
  at the outside
    jettying in.

        No walls, only a heap
    of dry, incinerated
      haemorrhage hopes,
thorny cacti, shrunken flowers,
    burnt grass, red leaves,
      cinders.

She started building
  once
    more
This time, not
  a home
    but a sky.

Of Mother and Trees

My Mother perhaps was born
    on the same day as Anne Frank

Anne saw the cherry blossoms
    dreamt of the chaste beauty of life
in cloistered darkness
    till life said good bye,

Her dreams were fulfilled
in the buoyancy of eternity.

My Mother planted her red hibiscus tree
    watered its roots daily

Added vital soil to nurture
    its soft growth and
save it from the burning sun
    while she always dreamt through drudgery.

Her dreams lived throughout her
full life, forever unfulfilled.

Stifled Scream

Her scream has travelled long
through the hollows of ages
in the whispers of dogma

A playful child she was at nine
with peals of laughter
kindling her cerise cheeks

Her dimples gleeful with her
clink of glass bangles holding
lovingly her slender wrists

The crackling jungles dim
the blossoming trees and foliage
all in sync with her whimpering giggles

While that foreboding heaved
deep within her childish bosom
with screams strangled by tradition

Soon her glass bangles broke
brittle like her silent weeping heart
her whole self enchained in gold

The young bride pushed into a maelstrom
of alien space walled in with her wails
in clandestine folds of her trousseau

An under creeper wrenched out of
her soil for gory transplantation
her shrieks now deep as the ocean

No dearth of kith and kin or friends
no dearth of relationships half baked
in-laws, children, grand children

Her lord in sunny glory of revamping her
Through decades, she in seeming command
as the screams pierce deeper into her loam

She remains forever the forgotten trophy
now a sudden horizontal marble white
the grand matriarch dressed up again

Her last journey as lavish, pallid and ashen
as that first one with gleams and shrieks
she the *Ma Durga* and her carcass floating now

Worship, immersion, festivity, facades
all drowned fading into memories and births
speaking silences of generations of women
in undeterred selfhood of throttled screams
dying every instant with their fortitude of dreams

Unborn Kill

I felt my throbs
deep within
the frothy warmth of
my mother's insides---

I was she
a teardrop on the serrated edge
of being,
a dew on her hidden, clement leaf
soon to be sucked out by
the boiling seas, the hot winds
of prejudice -----

I am not sure when
or how my mother
loved or wept
not sure whether
it was a blunder, a crime,
an accident
or perhaps moral turpitude -----

But sure enough
I wept with her in pain
while my instant was
blotted out under
the dark arc lights
in an ageless cry---

Sindoor

on that day of blood and tears
the rattle of conch shells
the red dust a looming cyclone
over the fences dividing my hair
sweeping through my soul of being
in a bridal ceremony of blinding smoke
of the caged goddess
a slip of a milk-white girl
daubed with *sindoor*
when a raging storm blew
across the depths of love
all so subterranean
in veil and vain
hidden in unknown warmth
an incalculable loss
of being free or not so free ---

somehow the *sindoor*
the colour of fire in the torpedo
matched the ambience
of that redness which rippled
like a wounded river through
the veins of wedlock
in dark cherry humour
of paraphernalia and festivity
clutters of rituals

heaps of clotted mire and
a lock bolted with unruly
miasma of emotions ---
a melange of strangeness
in joy and sorrow
in fondness and hate
in affection and affliction
trampled and tainted womanhood
with an unbreakable seal
the *sindoor* a dusty hallmark
indubitable yet bafflimg
its mercury fangs
pangs never understood
of an Indian bride wedded
to a groom with no such
badge or bondage of faith ---

not knowing though
a sea immeasurable
lay deep inside me
buried and unwanted
choked in the ashen grave
drowned again in the *Ganga*
our river of sacred liquescence
where carcasses of
the Mother Goddess float
with oodles of redness
crying spills of faith from
the *sindoor* ceremony
which just precedes
her inevitable immersion
in waves of incertitude
in a sea of doom---

Mother : A Memory

From body to fire
From prayer to rejection
From celebration to devastation
From love to oblivion
From royalty to rubbish
Each day, every day
The worship of *Durga* and *Kali*
We the idols in the playhouse of
Our mates, our tormentors, our devotees
Our canvasses painted
With sham vibrancy of display
Then rubbed off into
Paper-thin, watery, spectre-wan
Sheets of death ---

Drums, gongs, *dhaks, dhols*
Spell out through the *Navratris*
Days and nights celebrating the Goddess
Dressed in barren finery
Doomed to be pushed into
The *dashami* of the Ganga ---

Drifting in unloved rootlessness
Cadavers of brittle clay and straw
We God-Women with dismembered
Forms, spirits and bodies

Speed down the river of amnesia
On the final day
Proclaiming the Mother's victory in death ---

Fire and water
Elements, straw and slime
Phantom- attachments waylaid
Consume all our love
Embers dying with frail disconnect
Flesh of impalpable selves
In the last grey shreds of life ---

Our corpses of memory
Consigned to the flaming waters
Or enshrined indifferently in urns
Vacant tombs and mortuaries
 Smouldering with intense incense
Garbage in forgotten lofts
Hanging in parched photographs
Sometimes on crumbling walls ---

These shadows, ghosts of time
Nameless lances of limp motherhood
Cut across the breath of life
The ozone fails, the fluid stops
The mirror cracks forever
As her last gasps of coma
Dwindle within us
Into the approaching evanescence ---

Tinsel Heart

your stuffed tinsel-self
                your enamelled soul
          your silver facade
       forever rummages through
     the debris of my cries
    the winter leaves come and go
the seeds often die
   with the winds
      the after-hues of sunset
        puffed off to extinction
          with the morning dazzle
              non-cognizant of the ever present
other side of darkness---

my glowing stretches
              remain un-kissed
          un-cared for while your
       spikes bruise my body
      crush my breasts and
     smear my being
    my tears try to scale
   the skies
    drown the seas
      heave the geniality of the sun
        despite your
           razor-sharp treacheries
              always proving the loveless
baubles of your heart ---

The Divine Feminine

I shine in your translucent third eye
    Glimmering through my lows and highs
Nestled deep within my joys and sighs
    As the stars perform your blazing sacraments
I am your beaming face in ignited sanctity
    Changing with the seasons, seas and skies
In that universal rhythm of empathy and ire
       In the swirling deeps, the whirlpools of my soul
       Your refulgence a mirror of my cosmic whole
       Your vision in the diadems of my sight
       My angst in the swirling motions of your light
    Your changing multi-facets reflect our lives
Of wisdom and anger, of effusiveness and strife
    Your watery flaming face and self
So redemptive, transformative, regenerative
    Lucent Motherhood in my Self-blessed Womanhood
Like that invisibly embedded Holy Gyre
    I remain the Woman of your sacred Fire
Your strength, your Love my lustrous Power---

Veiled Chimera

I often see them ---

these dragon flies dreamy,
deluded, dazed in fiery glimmer
in oneiric existence
with slender frail bodies
of ornate wings in shimmer,
with entanglements seamy---

One a veiled lady chimera
poised between two dead ends,
droning on blank walls
odes of non-existence
in spider-nets of incandescence
filtering through the glass façade
with no possibilities
of exits or entries
through light or fire or glass
stuck forever in desires,
throbbing in simmers,
an artifact glorious
with enough motion
to die---

Moon Spindles of Singhbhum

weaving cane baskets, darning rags,
making coconut-brooms,
sun-drying dung cakes
stoking half-dead fires
      in wrapped up cracked huts
of murky loam along denuded roads,
is what they know of as destiny---

dented coal-tar, thrashed beaten corn,
wheat in meagre spread-outs
on the margins of highways
compose their muffled lives---

their nude children, progenies of darkness,
kick on the outskirts of life
prancing penumbras of remote light---

their black burnished bodies, shapely female figurines
heaving in sun-burnt labour,
picking up firewood or half rotten fruits
in deep pachyderm infested jungles---

born for back-breaking chores in devastated fields,
farms or homes for leasing themselves out to lazy,
lascivious males, owners or husbands in liquor stupor---

The moon steadily blinks on these tired horizons,
frayed indigenous spaces of *Singhbhum* or *Bethla*
yarning their stories on an endless spindle---

Eternal Mother

I rejuvenate life with blazing fire
I cause chaos with my awesome ire
I rinse the earth with raining thunder
Then placidly soothe in shower
Life's core of my fertile anger---

I am the soft water-hyacinth
And flaming red oleander
I am the rose of multi-hued satin
The white lotus of fleecy clouds
I embrace, kiss, cry and sing
With my weeping raging ember
There is none to equal me
In quenching your ache dire
Love, truth and justice
Revolve in my ageless gyre
For I am the Woman
I am the Mother---

I offer both light and shade
Plenty in my cumulus
I remain forever chastening
Your pivotal stimulus
I create and annihilate
In aesthetics of joy and pain
I am your high and low tide
In the vastness of my main!

Lakshman Rekha

Why did *Sita* cross the *Lakshman-Rekha*
(or did she trip over it ?)
between life and death,
that shrouded secrecy
between light and darkness---

that ultra-thin divide
between faith and longing---
that muslin-veil between
appearance and reality ?

Why did she pierce through
that cryptic, crystalline wall
stretching endlessly between good and evil
to meet her abductor half way ?
to pursue a golden deer
through an endless mesh of verdure,
through tunnels of silenced shrieks ?

Why did *Sita* throw herself away
to the winds and the deserts ?
to the skies and the rivers ?
rend apart her heart in glassy schisms---

trample upon her own jewels, her own creations,
her own crown of flowers ?

leave behind her own garden,
her own home, her own *aangan* ----

wrench in distressed pieces her own dreams, desires,
drapings, sarees, *ghunghat* in wreathed agonies,
show the fearful fissures engulfing her own self
in the grand finale of fire and tears --------

Was it to punish *Ravana*
or *Rama*?

Queen Nature

Queen Nature is on her way
to her regal bed with the blazing
red jewel in her crown softly sinking

This orbed central piece in dazzle
is about to be slipping into
the hidden depths of her closet

Her red attire splashed wildly with
the satin shades of multi-hued orange
dappled from the holy painter's palette

Our matriarch spreads across her universe
as she slowly disrobes with curtain-fall
while her royal trail still lingers in red haze

In her empyrean with the fading sheen
of her sun-gold crown darkness spills fast
gradually smearing her imperial gown

Spectral black engulfs her luminosity
while she is dazed by somnolence
the turbulent ocean tides roll in fury

Queen Nature sleeps in red oblivion
when hurricanes and floods trundle
and avalanches re-awaken her

Gone into the gradual deep in
sloping vales of the shimmering
sequined brume of her sleep

She rises again with bated breath and faith
the day breaks with her tangerine tenacity
her lucent orbed crown in naughty ploy

From the depths of the darkness
in Lethe to another splendid bathing
in the cream morn sparkling as herself

With our loyalty to Queen Nature
and our prayer-baskets soaked in ablutions
her healing returns with the emergent dawn

For nothing can stop her from arising
From a burial as fragile as naught
Yet soon she overtakes land, sea and sky!!

Red Rose Calling

Listen soulfully to
    the whistling rose
a red bride in crepe and satin
    the fresh florescence
of spring fire in a soft soul
    lovingly cuddled among
her bed of balmy leaves
    laughing with green dreams
kisses of nature's bounty
    with her open arms
for the beloved or in the
    cascading warmth of
a mother's embrace while
    she softly unfurls her
coy quivering petals with
    her deepest secrets in coitus
the blessed bees abuzz
    nestle in her amorous gaze
she glows with the soft touch
    of the coaxing foliage
in her bridal bower making
    this redness a chant aloud
of love's godly cadence
    with the echoing chords
of human essence---

      sooner than later
the boorish clutch throttles her
    she falls to ground in gory disarray
her requiem sonorous still in trance
    rising scent yet with her hymn everlasting---

Mother and Child in No Man's Land

Throwback to Corona Times

Last night the TV visuals
a lighted circle in a penumbra
froze me into numbness
as I viewed a frazzled migrant
mother with a stern leonine
gaze clasping her babe
in a loving kangaroo brace
positioned precarious on a jet-speed
buffer between perilous rails
as I slipped into a murky daze.

In endless restlessness
moving from side to side
between sleep and awakening
I saw that baby Jesus again
and again in an apocalyptic shine
snuggled in the arms of
the Mother weeping divine
in her purgatorial gloom
cradling her bleeding child
while I continued to be
arrowed in by a dark gleam.

The lost mother holding tight
her infant in her arms
a shroud perched dangerously
on the edge of Life in Death
and Death in Life snare
or perhaps an irrevocable
strangle-hold of cruel emperors
sitting afar in power zones
for making them aliens
in their own land damned forever.

Lost woman in wretchedness
still unafraid in fond grip and grit
since motherhood knows no hurdles
unshakeable through a tremorous
journey of timeless jeopardy
between railway tracks of furious haste
across deadly chasms in a
fearless but pitiful state of
in-betweenness, homelessness
hopelessness, rootlessness
jerking violently through a
no man's land to nowhere
in search of morsels or refuge
perhaps never to be found in
a land known to be her own.

Millions of her cursed tribe
follow her path of fatigued
never to end lost ways of hunger
disease or war-torn ravages
ruthlessly failed by those
they thought were their own

crawling death or unfound safety
cripples them cryptically
in this never-ending terminal zone
weary track of quest for crumbs
their begging bowls empty
hollow like those rhetorics
of promises never to fructify
while I sleep through this nightmare
of cycles of gloomy screenshots
myself a feverish mother in empathy.

As the sun rises I break off to see
my night-driven images actualized
in loud outcries with outstretched
hands for alms and food outside my gate
real sweat drenching them
in the sultry heat longing and
yelling for that which rightfully
belongs to them and their human kind
I run to the gate to give what I can
myself helpless as never before
      in this give and take.   …

I do not know what is in store
      for such vulnerability
as the Mother and Child
continue to haunt me
I question myself in these torn times
are they dead or just may be
resurrected in a new dawn
a scintillating distant one
a carol through the ages
which we still pray for!

Primordial Woman

I find you in the cosmic void of my being
when I tremor in the fury of ageless hurricanes
when an unforeseen apocalypse terrorizes
in labyrinths, caverns, surreal non-answers
I curdle an infant bud in your safe womb
growing to birth a mother in your universal placenta---

I find you in the rinsed vacuum of my being
while the world rotates in an unequal delirium
enwraps me in a swirling motion of darkness
when rivers get burrowed in sand and grime
as mountain glaciers thaw as blistering hellholes
I seek the cover of your cleaved bosom of warmth ---

My mother, I was born of you just as you of me
we are celestial twins out to revel and cure
warriors in the detritus of a putrid civilization
to create beauty from truth and love from hate
we rove the gardens of paradise gathering manna
and ambrosia for awakening the goddesses of heal---

I find you ever in the vigilant spirit of my being
in the fire and fragrance of our untold union
a mother born of another and of so many more
we the countless mothers of creation and cosmos
in the void of being, non-being, belonging and beyonding
our Motherhood and Womanhood a celebration of pain
the world needs to be baptized with ---

Fire of Yagnaseni**

I am queen *Yagnaseni*
born of pure sacred fire
love of the One and lust of many
a Fire Woman who destroys ignominy

I birthed from the fire of gods
soared into luscious beauty
the riotous flames draped me
in a shine of sacrificial chastity
the elements of the red and blue
hoisting my youth of multi-hue
wrapped around in silent agony
I remain the fiery *Yagnaseni*
love of the One and lust of many

I am a woman of the world
and a free soul of the skies
my sacred fire blazes and purifies
but I never was blessed with
the innocence of childhood
never was lured to catch the moon
nor ever felt the joy of kites or toys
nor the merry pursuit of balloons
but I am the warrior *Yagnaseni*
a Fire-woman who battles ignominy

I rove and dance with laughter
to ignite the fire of life
I am drunk with my flaming beauty
though untainted in being a wife
shared by five men of power
or dice-gods or spineless kings
eunuchs addicts or demons
in the royal courts and cloisters
of the palace of illusions which
my fire reigns with immaculate agony
I am the great *Yagnaseni*
love of the One and lust of many

as a princess and queen though
following my duties in the
imperial house often and more
my invincible fire takes me through
the stormy fearsome infinite jungle
though banished with my kingly men
I find their lost path in the dark tangle
I roam distressed as a beggar maid
still fierce with a vilified destiny
still looking for my Love amid the many
I am the ever constant *Yagnaseni*
I am fire who always fights ignominy

on that black day of an entrenched scar
unforgettable in my turbulent memory
injured bleeding myself dragged to court
engulfed in the silence of conspiracy
enmeshed unpardonably in history
as a royal woman to be raped with infamy
my fire leaps across desire and divinity

yearning for the loved One with searing agony
as He comes to wrap me in his embrace
and save my private space and grace
I remain the invincible *Yagnaseni*
the Fire warrior who combats tyranny

my fire singes boundlessly now but
I break open in the stretch of the high
I roar and drop like the thunderbolt
my sizzling lightning across the sky
in me the inferno of the heavens
which yearns for justice and chastens
at last my Love echoes my battle cry
with the reins of the chariot he hastens
with drums and conch shells to the war
I cry with the solace of my fiery star
appeased at last as *Yagnaseni*
love of the One and lust of many
the fire of creation and annihilation
I am the light of a thousand suns
burning in me as I remain *Yagnaseni*
the fire- slayer of a devilish destiny
created by Man through guiles so many
yet myself love of the One and lust of many
I remain forever Queen Yagnaseni---

** *Yagnaseni*---- Another name for ***Draupadi,*** the Chief Female Protagonist of the Indian Epic of the ***MahaBharata-*** -----symbolising Woman Power, Fortitude as well as Justice & Retaliation for the worst kind of ignominy from a Patriarchal Society, **Lord Krishna** being her only Saviour.

Red Bloom

I am a funnel-shaped red bloom
spruced in white innocence
in the placenta of hidden fire
embedded in my breathing seed
I remain a purity in mire
the moist loam my swaddle
as I sleep placidly in my soil
in warmth of my mother's womb ---

Soon spring arrives with dancing heels
pulls me out of my nascent cradle
in dissembling frolic as I flower
with my dreams of unbegotten love
but my colour of silken threads
erupts a sudden red volcano
flared by hate and lust with revival
all over clogged with blood- torrents
my redness to kill or be killed ---

Then I wane and fall to ground
my soul in dismay disarrayed
I kiss my parched Mother Earth
I become just a teardrop of strife
O I am uncared in the palm of life
a bubble in air about to fade away
in elusive smiles after all that fire ordeal ---

A ruddy hibiscus, a baby lost in smoulders
a future yet with slender hope of renewal
while my flaming genesis still evokes me
I am a red bloom never to become ashen
I am the red vibrancy of a pregnant woman
I hibernate to blossom and open up again
In the hallowed phallus of the dancing god
A celestial vagina in the garden of creation
to nestle in the arms of endless love
a genesis and prayer in our paradise!

Fireball

You wish
to catch the fireball
whirring in
the whispers of your insecurity,
spreading its balmy luminescence
deep in the darkness
of your hidden green shadows ?

You wish to tap
and trap it
in your small whirlwinds ?

The fireball rolls high and far
beyond and above
every black entrapment,
filling the heart and face
of every blossom
with the glitter of its soul,
with the resonance of
its sublime trumpets,
over and up and down
and far away.

Till you succumb to
its torpedo-strength,
its starry far-fetchedness.

In the dwindling sea-storm
the fireball catches you,
cleanses you,
scorns and lacerates you
with its own punitive red blaze.

Till you hold your washed flag
up to its canonized fire
of benign essence.

Devi – Manushi

I see you through my vigilant third eye to purge
with my mystic lustre your power-struck dirge
nuzzled in the cycle of raptures and sighs merged
I am in the luminous sun, moon, land and tides in surge ---

The spangled skies and lands sing my sacred ditty
blaze resonating through my incensed rhapsody
you will find my beaming face in everyday purity
through time, earth, firmament in elemental beauty ---

I change with the seasons yet I am the holy stasis
I destroy evil and bless good with haloed bliss
I breathe in the human, the divine and lazuline azure
I am the cosmic rhythm dancing in purifying anger ---

I am the churning whirlwinds in the nub of your soul
your incandescence a mirror of my multifold whole
my shifting yet constant features in your cyclical lives
I live in your every breath, every act, every vibe ---

I am the sleeping baby ensconced in your womb
I am your Mother too holding you till the tomb
I am the wrath of the storm, the cool of the blue
the telescopic transcendence of life's every hue ---

I am invisibly embedded in your sacred gyre
I save you ever from the demon's lusty ire
I am your sustenance, creation and annihilation
I am your source and goal of every regeneration ---

I am your progenitor, your milk-giver and much more
I am in your altar, your kitchen, in the poor girl at your door
I am Woman, Goddess, Strength, Love and Fire
I am She, I am He, I am your refulgent Mother ---

Grandma's Red Wrap

A fallen star from the skies
brave and romping in
the first flush of youth
bathed in milk whiteness
sparkling still on ground
with inspired choreography
of the heavens yet unaware
of her grandma's cloak around her ---

her dreamy eyes filled with
the founts of the Hippocrene
her soul gurgling with ablutions
the passionate bliss of brooks
the *Alakananda* gushing out
of its source in the wombs
of the Himalayan summits
pure billows down the vale of youth ---

a fierce energy spurting unbarred
she as clean and holy as the air
undeterred as the breeze
yet unknown to her future
to her grandma's dark cloak
still wrapped around her silently
through ages of furtive prejudice
in the redness of womanhood ---

marriage is a necessity she is told
yet not to the love she yearns for
but to a *Kulin* man from the uppermost
rungs of a cruelly segmented society
double or triple or many times her age
with enough shrewdness to ransack
her fancies, freedom and longings ---

soon her journey begins backward
into a mediaeval arena of dark red
or perhaps a stupor pinned in a lifeless bend
but with the bald zest of an old man
in a bridal chamber of incest and death
daily labour with nocturnal sleeze
her expected widowhood or her bleakness
of life in a dank room of loneliness ---

she goes back in temporal spaces
hears the murmurs buried inside
conspiring against those child widows
their grandmothers and mothers pushed aside
into secret funeral pyres, killed alive with deceit
as *satis* or sacrificial lambs in stranglehold
in the name of faith and unsullied femaleness
while she still hears their cries across meadows
across the immense ennui and galactic hollows
as she remains wrapped forever in her
grandma's dark cloak of red bondage in waiting ---

Blood Streams

Our blood stream floods incessant
in ageless stories of stealthy ferocity
through the craggy crevices in spurts
of bruised limbs, breasts and bodies
held to ransom in silken futile faith
soundless in the penitence of rocks
in sorrows unwept through ages
for acts that tear open the hibiscus
shattered and trampled roses on ground
red rivers satiate thumping maleness
as wails are choked in silent nights ---

I am one of you among so many
the race of mothers ravaged through
every particle of time and space
countless trees like us axed daily
parades of nakedness remorseless
perfidy with Nature peeling its colours
flooding red tears and coloured blooms deflowered
dragged, undressed and clawed
while red rivers gush unabashedly
earth soaked in injured cerise pawed
crimson crimes relentless against woman kind
Oedipus kings now are calcified brine ---

no gouged eyes, no handcuffs or noose
only wombs of genesis ruptured and annexed
sliced trees howling with cut open birth-holes

swathes of chilled red of icy blood
redness spilt and splashed in ruinous mess
in the festival of demoniac splashes
mother-less-ness yelling across torn skies
barren homes and deserted paths of barbs
ruddy rivers of lava overflow through sands
all violence over and across, beyond and above
killing mother earth our only refuge ---

Soul and Sham

The awry lounge my breath-taking sphere
where fashionistas, corporates and page three
crowds amalgamate with cheer and vaunting
they come and go, no, not talking of Michelangelo
but of themselves or opulent art exhibitions
in the Habitat or IIC or coffee-table books launched
in commodified creativity centres with myths
money of rising and falling shares with self-promos
more myths of mutual bonds and mercurial mammon
temporary as my lip gloss and gossamer red sari
my shimmering jewellery included, I am his prize
which is squeezed, kissed and shared
in slippery public spaces for climbing his ladder ---

O let us have some cocktails, mocktails, bloody marys
merri-go-rounds of rollicking spirits among bragging
handsome honchos hugging merrily mindless vanity
opaque selves romancing with see-through drapes
revealing breasts, sensuous waist lines and masked minds
like the red blush-on and concealer of dark flaky skins

One fumbles with some stale lines of poetry
as another sings a toxic off-tune song
and some discuss the next board meeting
with bitter halves of moving dolls in waylaid façades
this time for deciding male fate and corporate prices
while some confer about the upcoming club-extravaganza

I am pushed to the shifty floor by him
to dance with unknown casanovas
the festive fury mingles with the engulfing sham

I disentangle to run to my cubby hole soon
to make the bed comfy for that other one
as the stench of his alcohol burns my incense
I am brave in my sacrosanct shrine now
having borne the brunt of my perpetual awry dream
a cosmetic civilization of redness I rub off my lips
finally I rest in the snow-white beauty of my soul ---

Dark Red Spring

We play with dolls
and kites and ribbons
we soft teddies of playful blood
tumbling paper boats
we float in dripping ponds of frolic

soon we grow up or
are made to grow up
elasticity stretched in constriction
an approaching rusty winter
well before springtime arrives

marked like tame cattle
for the slaughter house
we in power-struck marriages
smudged in redness all over
ranks of flaming married women
widowed, sallow or virgin colourlessness

blotches, bruises, necklaces, stains
a conundrum of female chains
bedecked life one can never understand
emancipation a far cry of the ether

tentacles and cobwebs rummage us
tangles of masculine stink

sindoor and *mangal sutras*
bindis and bangles all of shackles
and then questions of wanton symbols
shredded freedom with approaching night
darkness with questions of chastity
the fire of the *Ram-Sita* story ongoing
alive in clandestine backyards

the sprit killed, senses mangled, body distraught
love a distant dream of never-land
daily chores and chaos in forced smiles
as he enters the bedroom to pound my earth---

Searching Home

Do I really have a home?
I am a tiny plant by the wayside
breathing heavily while trampled upon
I find a place then in the garden of kindness

that little girl grows up with me in fondness
sometimes under the cool shade of a tree
sometimes pulled out painfully or lovingly

uprooting causing more agony
than my birthing from my lost mother
often in blood, shrubs, spikes or thorns

I pulsate with the young woman now
a bridal home she finds away from home
or in a land far away from her own

I am a migratory bird of penance for no sins
though for me all else is impermanent
I am a shuttle cock played between sides
father, husband, son, lover or brother
tenderness in partnership vacillates as I move
a soft and mute plant can always be
dislocated and planted and relocated again
in alien bushes or a hedged defensive garden
with new journeys, new chores, new kins

new habitats, new foods, new clothes
new agendas but my own mauled soul
with a home here and a home there
another near or another far away
like the moving orioles and planets
roving through the galaxies
of motions in an ethereal vacuum

I move from this home to another
never settled, I still look, I still move
in search of my home

yet in the translucence of sudden love
I silently canoe to that island
very far from that customary red volcano
a hug of green love in the crystalline blue
where I now hope to find my home ---

Woman or Wood Nymph

My tracks never touched
each other

they crisscrossed, bifurcated
or ran longingly parallel

my azure skies were never kissed
jilted by my red horizon

my cerulean midnight blue never spread
its arms to my torn, worn out edges

my moon in its lambent hue dangled
a lonesome piece in grey clouds

radiating apathy and pallid glory in
a lustreless dream light

which blanched, etherized my skin
and robbed its warmth

my sun never blessed my stars
a careless, distant fireball

it shone afar ever ready to scald
to singe my yearning soul

my rain never inundated me though
I waited to bathe in its shimmering showers

they came and went like watery splinters
with cold fake priestly rituals

with ardour more to drown
than to rejuvenate

here I am at last a decorative figurine
lost in red rituals

more a wood nymph
than a woman.

That Red Glistening Edge

The veiled hue of my organza *ghunghat*,
    The muted sheen of my nail enamels,
The blurring sundown of my lip gloss,
    The stifled glitz of a caked make-up,
No longer lures me to your shadowy enclave
    Of fraudulent dreams---

    My dusky kohl eyes have dimmed
    With the knowing of life
Now embedded in the hallowed hues
    Of the blues and whites of untouchable holiness
While the soft scents of my bosom rise
    Like the smoky spirals of smothering incense
The distant under-tonal rhapsody of the hills
    Vales, skies and cataracts resonate
With my tinkering anklets tuned to that unknown
    Drum and lyre playing beyond evanescence
Often fading into a cloudy stillness of loss
    My dark tonsured curls now accommodate
In gleeful waves this new life
    Of explosion, expansion and red vision---

Your sapphire empyrean, emerald oceans,
    Carnelian horizon, rosy love,
        Incandescent butterflies, energizing breeze,
            Aromatic blooms, blinking glow-worms

           Kaleidoscopic multi-hued gardens
                Like my fragile glass bangles---

Circulate
Activate
Simulate
Break
        On the periphery
        Of the penultimate zone---

            Hovering around that pivotal area I search for
                    Far away from shrines
            From prayer
        From faith
            From benediction
        From hope
From hopelessness
        From delusion
From extinction---

    The dull pink horizon stretches out
        To the thin films of the deepening night
            While the hide and seek sunrays peep
                At the red glistening edge
                    Of that ruby which soon fades in treason

        I wait as life goes on
    I wait as always for the answer
    As always, one thumb away from my clutch---

Roses Arise

(On a Painting by Edouard Manet)

You see through my translucence
My soul of watery innards
A green yearning for a palette
Of our special communion

Rippling cascades of placidity
So often erased or assaulted
In a niche of unnoticed beauty
That flies in the ether of love

I come to you through eons fragile
In the air of my flagrant intensity
Splashing like the currents on shore
Perhaps its tranquillity in the horizon

I become an angel with winging roots
My slumbering self in vermillion liquidity
Splurging with elemental bliss of ditties
Verdure embracing my red in our elysium

Rainbow hues in the sky of red roses
Painted azure of the blooming garden
Bleeding refractions rising in my longing for you
Ascent in my art of grim loftiness

Strange Parting

As my last rites are over
You sink into a fractured cosmos
A sodden sadness unprecedented
A sudden warmth never before
Enclosed in time and space yet spilling away
Walking in dribble of the dreams of yesterday
With the ashen remembrance of my songs
Still unsung, longings still unfelt and unsaid
Tightly sealed within your lips
As in that urn, your guile-laden treasure trove
Placed in front of my hanging self
Now on the painted wall of garlands
A piece of dwindling meaning
A ritual after a lifetime
Of strange partnership
In the vacuous home décor
Or perhaps in the silence of reminiscences
Between the known and unknown ---

The setting sun muted in fury
Still blazes in the funeral pyre of your eyes
The reddened fountain of your tears
Too human to be lauded or reprimanded
The dark skies die with the ruddy daylight
A fisherman struggles in his boat unsure
To return home only as an unknown speck

Engulfed in the void of the bruised horizon
A tiny minuscule of incertitude in unruly seas
You now sit in your lonely corner of ruminations
Brooding of love or hate that never was
Moments of bliss or bitterness
Unravel on the slow screen of your mind
As *Ragas Pilu* or *Kirwani* or *Darbari* play
In your melancholic symphony
Unusual in this resonance of sudden loss
In the courtyard of our insipid story ---

Here and now there is no more certainty
Of meeting or loving or living or parting again
I am a non-entity floating ember in the elements
My home and self now, as ever, in a conundrum
Of unfulfilled promises and unrequited love
In lost half-ways and unsolved half-truths
A tyranny of sorts has overtaken me and you
With unresolved questions and incomplete bonding
My womanhood a riddle and your perspective a cruel quiz
In this automation of life called animation
Where inanimate destiny rules, runs and ruts
With society in riveting momentum
On a speedboat not driven by you or me ---

As late as yesterday you finally opened your heart for me
But I closed my eyes for it was already late and time for me to go
Sailing beyond to that never-land of no recovery
My child, books, harmonium, tamboura all waylaid behind,
My silks, gems and perfumed enchantments
Our soirees and those decorative bejeweled pieces
Of bonhomie and rocking get-togethers all redundant

As it always was in dreary dailiness of futility---
Now a scene of empty decorum
Now violent tinges and sporadic kindness
Swept away by sudden winds of oblivion
Now nothing seems real except the shoreline
The regrets and memories of our history washed off
Myself a memory of remnant baggage
Attenuating on the bleeding horizon
Stacked away in your red clammy attic
Locked out forever
Framed in wooden amnesia---

Cigarettes

you smoke us
every night
we your cigarettes
      the burnt out
butts flung into bins
never to be picked up
again

we remain unknown
to you
to ourselves
      in the smoky spirals
in the flare of
your worn-out
lascivious passions

we are your cigarettes
that need to be banned
for life
      for our very own sake
for the red fire that
scorches us out to the farthest
end of our fruitless nights

we suffer in self-immolation
in so-called love

in lost simmering identity
        with aching swan songs
sweltered in tangles of your dead wood
though you have smoked us out
into pallid nothingness and celebrated
your own scavenging manhood
        in your upbeat vacuity

we too have eaten deep into
your vitals and flung you out
to ceaseless death
        with our power of self-redemption---

Scarred Moon

The moon-scars struck you from afar
you never looked closely for its light in darkness
you swayed comfortably in your boat
you counted the waves indolently playing flute
yet never swam or soaked in the river's finesse.

You spent sluggish days smelling scent of the rose
never peeped into its velvety heart of tenderness
spent your time in league with the honey bees
till she was shorn and axed from her stem of life
yet you never felt the ache of her fleeced soul.

You unveiled the bride in your amorous bed
made her fulfill her doormat-womanliness
a laurel of adornment in your lounge of laxity
weighed down with chores and everyday games
yet you had no time to hear her stories of angst.

You saw her daily in heaps of black coals
raw bindings which simmered every moment
her coal had to burn red to keep your warm hearth
so many words unsaid faded in her fissured self
yet you never embraced that diamond light
quivering through her wincing darkness of fire.

Womanhood

Look through the detritus to find them
They traverse on radically diverse lands
with brown, black, mixed or white surfaces
but with similar insides of blazing anguish
battered souls with moist red eyes shine in periphery
or those similar sprinkles of fleeting laughter
that allures through a short magical spell ---

They walk on river sides wide apart
lands on the west, east, north or south banks
yet in the same riverine waters calm or flooding
be it the Ganga, Danube, Hudson, Bosphorus or Nile
they still have the same stillness and rose-fury
the same wounded hunger raging in tender hearts
maelstroms circulating ever around the tranquil core ---

They are the flying kites dreaming awhile in rest
and restless freedom in empty skies with no goals
phantasmagoria of flaming rainbows of life
their hopes and jubilation cut short soon
as they hang in trees or lie cold on ground
they hallucinate the sun, moon and stars
with no balm for decorated jagged lives
grovelling in graveyards of lost gardens ---

The mini-skirted white one with unstable stilletoes
driven off with no home but a barrenness to fend
for herself in finding bread, education or shelter
the brown one is pushed off to marital rape or drudgery

for subsistence often in dreary fearsome quest
for her much awaited love with final heartbreak
of ex-communication, abuse and loneliness
while the dark black one becomes food for
bestiality, ravage, burden of parents and hordes
of siblings, all pushed to the margins for ages ---

Soon the church bells ring for Mother Mary
Conch shells are blown for Ma Durga and Kali
Festivals and carnivals held in empty celebrations
Uphill and downhill, the sameness of it all
The newly begotten Woman Power still boosts Patriarchy
Truce is another word for fraud in another new garb
A degenerate civilization clapping in a circus
Awaiting annihilation!

Red Queen of Nemesis

I am the red queen born of Nemesis
I have travelled through those
entrails of harshness surging softly
in my mother's soul and womb
a forbidden love story as always aglow
with that red fire which gave me birth
a red hibiscus in the fragile birth-hole
a blooming redness of raging petals
with five slivers of the fountain of creation
forever wedged in frays of aloneness
agog with stunning tremors of fear
of beauty withholding still the sunset cascades
in my blushing cheeks of tinted fire
suffused with glory and shame
a red girl cleansing the reluctant dawn
a rose and a hibiscus bathed in red scent
in blood-soaked rivers of cries unheard
I am still the red girl born of Nemesis ---

I prance in red whirls of my incensed spirit
yet draped in the heavy mesh of prohibition
the red *banarasi* a clinging robe handed down through
generations of female traditions brutally knotted
for the outlawed womanly gait through gates
a signature sari of thwarted redness
my muffled self unable to spread wings

or fly with my dainty feet timelessly
bound in grieving jingles of clangs
red bonds hindering boundlessness
traversing oceans of cruel liquescence
of crimson *altaa* smearing my every step
through the milky blood streams flooding
my dreams and gory doorways
to the inner cave of calling duties
as a red bride I enter with unawareness
ignorant of the black claws of redness infinite
as I remain the red girl born of Nemesis ---

and then the final ceremony of birth and death is complete
between golden chains, silver manacles and clinking bells
my handcuffs of bracelets reminders of a life of clutches
my diadem a crown of thorns of the imperial domain
my being of redness to be offered to the dumb gods
those wanton ones who were made forever libertines
to play with red girls, their duty-ridden minds and bodies
to pluck those red blossoms and tear the petals apart
for the soil to suck them into sobbing infamy or ignominy
their hair-partings wailing with blizzards
and billows of over-brimming redness
in loads of *sindoor* poured with that insignia
of treacherous pathways dragging me
blindfold with non-chalant faith forever cheated
yet I am the red girl born of Nemesis ---

but see how I rise from the ashes of my eruption
I break open the gates of the red sky at sundown
I look at myself the frail vagina of a hibiscus turned rock
I get ignited with the fire of a millennia of injustice

a spiraling crescendo of love in ruins
a shredded sky of spangled stars with weeping red
my redness now a volcano unfurling in the sky
exploding through dogma, delusion and deceit
I am now my final incarnate of Ma Durga, Ma Kali
and the unconquerable Whore of Love
as my laughter and outcries rend through
the realms of the unjust multiverse in wisdom
in the intangible forces of pain, loss, victory and history
I am now at last the Red Queen born of Nemesis ---

Memories

Memories, memories, memories
fleeting in stasis yet ingrained slivers
feathery flaps tipple in burning dust
in cryptic folds of fluidity and brittleness
moments of deep-seated frailty
flowing through fierce waters
my sailing paper boats unseen
squabble through rivers of the open heart
ripples and tendrils of the mind
cataracts running downhill
or lotuses in still meditative ponds
now soothing all seething red
in calm quiver of undying minuscules
snapshots of life etched in eternity ---

I know you wait forever
on the other side of my nostalgia
through the crimson flames
of azure kisses in reluctant ardour
my lighted horizon ignites
the waves of the ocean
offering their female bosoms
to the fierce inconstancy of love
so many crowded memories in blaze
the liberty of unknown kites in uncharted ways

and jubilant balloons momentarily resuscitated
in the unsure air of the mind
fireflies playing in torn silks
waver through flaming threads
of artists' cobwebs in ethereal fragility
snapshots of life etched in eternity ---

Dreams of hot *tandoori* evenings
quiet, steaming or cooling fantasies
crushed strawberry creamy beds
remembrances varied crafted inside
with a sculptor's glorious harshness
often the red presides over multi-shades
spirit of somnolence opening out at last
for the caged birds to fly off
between the arteries of space
between heaven and home
finding bowers and corners
of solitude across unending expanses
with liquidity of solace and ache
framing pictures in the universal void
unavoidable beauty and truth so true
silence and mesmerizing cacophony
memories live their own being
as the fireplace crooning in winter
and spring moving towards summer
motions of an unstoppable journey
inevitable ongoing of my rosy memory
snapshots of life etched in intangibility---

Nirbhaya

(To the Raped Daughters of India)

**The cold night of 16*th* December 2012 saw the ruthless Gangrape and consequent Death of the young Jyoti Singh symbolically named Nirbhaya or the Unafraid, who battled till the last moments of her life yet died and sent shudders throughout India. Though the Rape Laws became much more stringent yet the Rapists were hung after more than seven long years with such Crimes against Women still unabated till date.

her voice awakens us
   a thumping soft echo rings in our welded hearts
   a falling star, an erupting timelessness
despite the hooded darkness
   her sparkling absence
  becomes our magic wand
on the road to freedom

she is here and now
   she is you and me
     within and around
she is everywhere
   across and beyond the rainbow
   underground and overground
our *Durga, Lakshmibai,* our resurrected *Ahalya*

she ignites my question, your question
the question of countless Indians
wailing against that hapless Midnight
of our dubious tryst with destiny

the ardour of a thousand blazing moons
    the sprouting green lava after her shrieks
        have whetted myriad bleeding struggles
have sanitized our skies and seas
we are joined in worship in an endless cavalcade
    to redeem her unafraid volcanic tremor
resolved again to seek answers

Nirbhaya's sleeping voice is sleepless today
    with the lurking beasts still preying through
        our streets, our homes, our very own spaces
our cacti-forests are on fire
    our ravaged gardens seek justice
    our aridities yearn for *Nirbhaya's*
cool clear water and pure ire

we face each other, for each other
    linked in this encounter of
        prayer with folded hands
in a caravan of peace
    to the promised land
    perhaps to arrive or never to
with *Nirbhaya's* surging symphony

her fuelling soul hopes for a new dawn
amid the outrage against that
                celebrated Midnight of Mahatma's India

Denouement

And then the denouement comes after all
When the red spurs and finally blurs across the galaxies
After the red soil mixes and weeps with the bloodstreams
Whimpers of duress become rainbow smiles of the soul
After the rain- daggers have opened the foamy heart into newness
After the hand stretches far into emptiness to touch another
To repair, restore, remorse, fulfill and remedy the soft marble
Through all lawless floods of white and red gone haywire
And then the denoueument comes after all ---

After the chaos of the night mollifies the red spills
After wintry storms have left the trees pristine nude
After the young bride wings away into a lost, better world
After sterility fosters birthing of legions of women
Self-evolved, self-enlightened and self-created beings
After the boiling cauldron has sculpted beauteous youth
After the red credo has awakened the red girl to life
And then the denouement comes after all ---

After the charade of unflinching violence is over
And rigour of defenceless duties clinched
The red evening sky sheds its fiery red arrows
And mingles with the night with hope of sinking in
The cradle of a cuddled dawn as I slowly rinse in the sea
The red lotus transmutes into its effusive garment of aerial

light
The dribbling injuries of past redness heal with incantations
Translucence is born with that unforgettable red in a mélange
Of human truth and beauty in unshackled adornment ---

Look the red vagina is now a white rose of celestial grandeur
All redness purified and rejuvenated in my milky swan
Ferreting in unbound sacredness across stellar space
And then the denouement comes through timeless annals
To unfetter and release all taints and tints of trajectories
Erasing borders of dilemma between fertility and futility
As the skies and seas merge with the rolling multiverse
The Red Woman rises beyond the swirling clouds above
She is now the Mother of Ascension from the depths of love
Animated abandon of zephyrs in her unbarred freedom
And the denouement comes after all surmounting
It comes and it comes as it must come after all that---

(Copyright@Laksmisree Banerjee, 2024)

A Special Tribute to Womanhood

(In painful memory of a Global Protest/ Social Revolution against the Brutal Rape & Murder of a Female Doctor in RG Kar Hospital, Kolkata, India on 9th August----Universal Movement of Justice for Women Reclaiming their Rightful Space across Societies & Communities,2024)

The Desecrated Mother

that night the shimmering fuzzy stars
hid themselves in fear and shame
as did the night while watching
the monstrosity of the dark game---

the bleary eyed Mother wept and wept
with tears of endless riverine blood
are these the goons I gave birth to
soaked in such pernicious flood?---

they walked in with hate and lust
wrapped in mantles of murk and evil
they besmeared the motherly bond holy
with claws and paws like the devil---

they throttled, raped and ripped her apart
with inhuman torture in caverns of stress
as darkness wished to hide in the dark
to run away from being such a witness---

intoxicated with blind Dionysian fury
they forgot their mother in their black soul
they forgot the warmth of her lap and milk
as they defiled their Genesis whole---

yet who was she of many wounded like us
was she a *Draupadi* or an innocent *Ahalya*
was she a *Lucrece* or an unfortunate *Leda*
one among us reared with love's nectar---

or was she the Crusader full of Truth's ambrosia?

now she is both a living death and deadly life
a volcano, conflagration, unstoppable fighter
she is ready now to erupt with dire fire
to avenge and heal with the Mother's ire---

she is now our ignited Womanhood, an invincible *Abhaya*!

Unhappy Independence Day
(15th August, 2024, India)

let us not sing songs of freedom
let our flag unfurl in shame and pain
splinters of the mother's flesh
haemorrhage in blooms that wane ---

the heart has become shredded
with grey shrouds in prison maze
fuzzy and moist among crowds
who have forever lost their ways ---

in labyrinths of monstrous claws
among catacombs of lust and crime
where mothers drip deep in blood
daughters and sisters in shivers whine ---

no you cannot wash the blood away
you cannot cleanse your souls of gore
your hearts are brutal without tears
your hands and spaces in grimy sore ---

the vaults of history resonate with fear
in what freedom song would you sway
when womanhood is so lacerated
why and how celebrate Independence Day?

the searing agony with shackles of terror
have blocked your fraudulent way
whatever may be your white-wash hymn
when countless *Abhayas* killed and raped
do not flag or chant Independence Day!

Renaissance After her Martyrdom

After her martyrdom
see how birds of fire fly across the azure
and verdant fields shudder with quakes
the ocean rampages with red anger
the truth of stormy hearts of love in motion
connecting the deep rumbling thunder in shock
the rage of humanity bursting in cactus blooms
an upsurge, a social rebellion despite gloom
of mushroom clouds beyond redemption ---

After her martyrdom
under the debris of perfidy through time
through the bruised bodies and minds
of the one now transformed to so many
blood rivers of mothers hapless in explosion
now about to rise with the crescendo of passion
the female body and soul strewn in gory shards
now in the rubble of a degenerate civilization
now in the sphere of a weeping evolution
all prepared to break open the shackles
no way this upheaval will ever stop
till a new awakened sun rises in tearful blossom ---

After her martyrdom
all hazy except the smearing blood in deluge
from the womb and soul of womanhood in revolt

heralding all peoples beyond race, creed and colour
ushering in a new dawn of arousal unstoppable
a renaissance unveiling flags of freedom ---

After her martyrdom
the raped and murdered woman rises with angels
to strangle taint and treachery till avenged
till the cinders of her burnt fire blow in the wind
till every woman has sculpted grit from her ribs
till fists are ready to combat subjugation
till insurrection births from her funeral pyre
till all open highways and secret byways are sealed
and patriarchy asphyxiated with blasts of Justice
till Night, Day and the Universe is reclaimed ---

We Rise with Her

The torpedo has taken root in the soil
Yet her redemptive rainbow is visible on the horizon
See the skies bleeding with her tears
Tsunamis rage in a ceaseless plummeting spree
As she floats in the ruddy ocean of atrocities
Bacchic winds in her flailing limbs uproot
All covert crimes of monsters of the morgue
Her wails in voracious silence rend purgatory
The evil doers lanced in this apocalypse of sin
Avalanches hurl through infernos of freedom flags
Unfolding the deadly flames of stifled life
Universe rails in fury for justice of the Mother's race
No, we cannot stop till the seeds flower again
Till the verdure of love sprouts in redressal
Till the Womb stops bleeding in this demoniac carnage
We cannot stop till our noose has killed her death
We will not stop till we reach the foliage of humanity
We now await appeasement of a new daybreak
Till the pinnacle of our revolution cures diseased patriarchy
Till the gentle plenitude of Life wipes crimson tears
Her spirit of truth is restored for a genial posterity
As we rise with her, our *Abhaya* the fearless one---

GLOSSARY

- Sonagachi, Soho, De Wallen, Reeperbahn Strasse, Mello, Heeramandi, Kamathipura-------Famous Red Light Areas of the World
- Ardhanarishwar------ androgynous half woman half god (in oral traditions of Hindu liturgy)
- Brahmadaitya------- half god half demon (in oral traditions of Hindu liturgy)
- . unoons-----clay ovens
- Nondon kanon-------garden of paradise
- Lakshman-Rekha-- a forbidding line of chastity for women
- alta & mehendi ----decorative red colours for hands and feet of Indian Women as insignia of marriage
- havelis-------mansions
- bindi-----red dot on a woman's forehead
- sindoor----red vermillion—mark of an Indian married woman
- mantras-----chants or hymns
- Rama, Lakshman,Sita------deified protagonists of the Indian epic Mahabharata
- Ma Durga-----immersion--- ceremony of the clay image of the Mother Goddess thrown into the river after worship
- Alakananda---- source of the river Ganga in the Himalayas
- Hippocrene-- fountain of poetic inspiration in Greek Mythology
- Sati-----connotations of a chaste woman and also of the ancient Indian practice of throwing a young woman into the funeral pyre of a husband

Black Eagle Books

www.blackeaglebooks.org
info@blackeaglebooks.org

Black Eagle Books, an independent publisher, was founded as a nonprofit organization in April, 2019. It is our mission to connect and engage the Indian diaspora and the world at large with the best of works of world literature published on a collaborative platform, with special emphasis on foregrounding Contemporary Classics and New Writing.

www.ingramcontent.com/pod-product-compliance
Lightning Source LLC
Chambersburg PA
CBHW021627080526
44585CB00013BA/828